W9-DBU-495

DISCARD

CHICAGO ARCHITECTURE
1885 TO TODAY

EDWARD KEEGAN
FOREWORD BY LYNN J. OSMOND

CHICAGO

ARCHITECTURE

1885 TO TODAY

UNIVERSE

CHICAGO ARCHITECTURE FOUNDATION

First published in the United States of America in 2008 by
UNIVERSE PUBLISHING
A Division of Rizzoli International Publications, Inc.
300 Park Avenue South, New York, NY 10010
www.rizzoliusa.com

ISBN-10: 0-7893-1533-5
ISBN-13: 978-0-7893-1533-5
LCCN: 2007908775

Photography credits: see page 222.

FRONTISPIECE	Hyatt Center
FOLLOWING PAGES	Macy's State Street
TITLE PAGE	333 Wacker Drive
PAGE 11	The Rookery
PAGE 13	Contemporaine
PAGE 15	Carson Pirie Scott & Co.
PAGE 16	Jay Pritzker Pavilion

Designed by Abigail Sturges

Printed and bound in China

2008 2009 2010 2011 2012/ 10 9 8 7 6 5 4 3 2 1

Contents

Foreword

Chicago is the ideal place to begin an exploration of the modern metropolis. The pursuit of commercial opportunity made the "city on the prairie" a hub of industry during the nineteenth century. Unprecedented growth brought Chicago international renown as the archetype of an ambitious, diverse urban environment.

After fire leveled much of the city in 1871, the architects, engineers, and industrialists who converged here produced masterpieces of design. The work of legendary Chicago-based architects such as Louis Sullivan, Daniel Burnham, and Frank Lloyd Wright inspired architects around the world. Community activists and social science innovators like Jane Addams and Robert E. Park used Chicago as a laboratory as they pioneered new ways of understanding urban centers and city dwellers.

Within fifty years, three-quarters of the world's population will live in urban environments far denser than Chicago's. Addressing climate change and energy supply is essential to our survival and wellbeing. Architectural and urban design will help determine if our cities can become inclusive and sustainable. Exploring the buildings of Chicago is a starting point for thinking about what we want from our communities—and how to rebuild for the future.

The Chicago Architecture Foundation (CAF), founded in 1966, is a model for architecture centers worldwide. Through its focus on Chicago's architectural legacy, CAF promotes understanding of the built environment. We offer a comprehensive range of activities, including tours, exhibitions, lectures, special events, and youth and adult education programs. CAF challenges audiences to understand how architects, engineers, and planners shape our lives, and how each of us might participate. Our youth education programs are transforming how design is taught to students across the country.

Through public and private initiatives, our city is again at the forefront of urban innovation. The Chicago Architecture Foundation is proud to play a vital role—ensuring that Chicago will continue to be a model of the livable twenty-first-century city.

Lynn J. Osmond, Hon. AIA
President
Chicago Architecture Foundation

Introduction

Buildings have always been a little more important in Chicago. This fact starts in the very nature of the place. Simply stated, it is flat. A building—any building—makes a distinct mark upon the unbroken horizon. Since the city's incorporation in 1837, architects and builders, developers and real estate speculators have all conspired to replace its paucity of natural wonders with a man-made place of remarkable diversity and interest.

Chicago's uninteresting topography is mitigated by its fortuitous geography. In the wilderness that was the early United States of America, natural waterways were the easiest method of transportation. Chicago's advantage lay in its immediate access to the east via the Great Lakes and the south via rivers leading to the Mississippi. Early railroads stretched westward over the plains and made Chicago the hub of commerce for the entire nation.

If location and transportation pointed commerce in Chicago's direction, the Great Fire of 1871 brought architects and engineers. A talented few, including William Le Baron Jenney, already called the city home, but an entire generation soon beat their path to the newly emerging metropolis. Daniel Hudson Burnham, John Wellborn Root, Louis Sullivan, and Frank Lloyd Wright came from near and far to make their mark upon the flat city on the lake. The burgeoning commercial district that would be dubbed the Loop sparked an incredible flurry of invention by these figures and their brethren.

The 1893 World's Columbian Exposition placed Chicago firmly in the roster of international cities while establishing a local legacy for classically inspired architecture that still exists side by side with more technically derived design. The 1938 arrival of Ludwig Mies van der Rohe, a middle-aged international talent who led the progressive Bauhaus earlier in the decade, enriched the city's legacy and sparked a new period. The work of these Chicago architects and their colleagues reached most corners of the planet during the twentieth century.

For much of a century, Chicago's influence radiated outward, its best work (with a few notable exceptions) that of its native or adopted sons. In recent decades, there has been a more noticeable reciprocity. International stars such as Frank Gehry, Rem Koolhaas, Tadao Ando, and others have built in Chicago. Architectural ideas in a global age of instant communications are less likely to be tied to a specific place or even a single individual. Chicago's architects continue to build—and build well—along the shores of a big lake. Sustainability is a new concern, and the city's architects, prodded in this case by local government, are leading once again.

Presenting Chicago's architectural legacy in forty-two buildings is daunting. Dozens of extraordinary structures, many world-renowned, have been left out. These forty-two have been chosen for their quality as well as their ability to present the breadth, width, and depth of the city's remarkable built legacy.

The land is still flat, but the landscape no longer is.

Glessner House

Henry Hobson Richardson, 1885–87
1800 South Prairie Avenue

Boston architect H. H. Richardson was a large man whose girth reflected his appetite and influence. His Glessner House is a fortresslike home whose heavy granite walls forcefully express the power of nature.

During the 1880s, Prairie Avenue became an elegant South Side enclave for the city's elite. Richardson created a strong dichotomy when he employed a U-shaped plan at the corner of Prairie and Eighteenth. Rough-cut gray granite exterior walls promote privacy with their small window openings. A brick-faced interior court, accessed via a carriageway, has large windows facing south to allow ample sunlight into the house.

The two street facades reflect different functions. On Prairie, a tall slate roof tops the principal family living spaces. Its shallow arched doorway is surrounded by symmetrical window openings that set the formal entrance to the complex. In contrast, the long Eighteenth Street facade is asymmetrical. A deeply recessed arch—the building's signature motif—accesses the servants' quarters and ancillary uses.

The exterior displays little ornament. A few abstracted columns separate windows, and a checkerboard pattern of masonry protects the basement windows. The carefully arranged granite stones provide their own sophisticated narrative of nature—a balance between sedimentary heaviness and carefully protected domesticity.

Richardson died in 1886, before the completion of the Glessner House. It is the sole survivor of three buildings he designed in Chicago, including the Marshall Field Wholesale Store. His ideas and buildings deeply influenced local architects, including Louis Sullivan, John Root, Daniel Burnham, and Frank Lloyd Wright. They synthesized Richardson's strong architectural forms into a new, distinctly American architecture while transforming the city from the ashes of the 1871 Great Fire to a world-class metropolis during the latter decades of the nineteenth century.

19

Auditorium Building

Adler & Sullivan, 1887–89
430 South Michigan Avenue

The Auditorium Building was designed to be a virtual city within the city. Its original configuration combined a theater seating 4,200, a four-hundred-room hotel, and 136 offices and stores. The room that gave the half-city-block complex its name—the Auditorium Theatre—remains a sublime creation of Dankmar Adler's structural and acoustical genius and Louis Sullivan's aesthetic mastery.

Adler and Sullivan were already acclaimed architects of theaters in Chicago when they received the commission for the Auditorium. Sullivan developed several versions of the design, the final one strongly influenced by H. H. Richardson's recently finished Marshall Field Wholesale Store. A three-story base of rusticated Bedford limestone supports a four-story arcade. Two further arched stories topped by a single-floor attic complete the main block. A tower along Congress marks the entrance to the theater and provides additional floors of office space with panoramic views. Adler and Sullivan took the top floors of the tower for their own offices upon the building's completion.

The theater interior remains a marvel. Its exuberantly ornamented arches telescope from the stage and wrap the audience in Louis Sullivan's gilded vision of a new, authentic American architecture.

Other notable interiors include the hotel lobby (now Roosevelt University's main entrance off Michigan Avenue) and Rudolf Ganz Memorial Hall—originally a banquet hall for the hotel. Ganz Hall occupies a seventh-floor space between the tall trusses that span 120 feet across the Auditorium. Sullivan created a series of square piers topped by ornately carved wood capitals of his own design (each different) to support an arcade that frames the room.

The young Frank Lloyd Wright served as a draftsman for Sullivan on the project.

The Rookery

Burnham & Root, 1888
209 South LaSalle Street

Development of new structural systems for large urban buildings accelerated at great speed in the second half of the 1880s, and Chicago architects kept pace with aesthetic solutions to match. John Wellborn Root's design for the Rookery is highly eclectic and reflects the curious amalgam of stone, brick, iron, and steel that went into its supporting structure. Classical columns, Moorish motifs, Byzantine elements, and even whimsical carved birds from which the building takes its name can be found within the eleven-story facades facing LaSalle and Adams.

The elevation is developed in five layers. Two-story granite columns with rusticated stone piers at the corners and two arched entries facing the streets form the base of the building. The third and fourth floors are simply expressed in red brick with thin lintels. Floors five through seven sit within arched openings that recall H. H. Richardson's Marshall Field Wholesale Store, which stood only one block to the west along Adams Street. Eight through ten are almost a carbon copy. Elaborately detailed terra cotta ornament sandwiches the eleventh-floor windows to create a strong cornice with relatively shallow surface detail.

The building fills its almost square site. Root created a central light lined with large windows to provide natural illumination for all offices within the structure. White, glazed terra cotta walls reflected sunlight to the glass skylight of the two-story center court. Surrounded by shops and topped by an elaborate iron structure, this interior has been remodeled several times since the building's construction. Its current incarnation combines the designs of both Root and Frank Lloyd Wright. The shallow urns that flank the ceremonial stair are part of Wright's 1905–07 scheme.

Second Leiter Building

William Le Baron Jenney, 1889–91
403 South State Street

William Le Baron Jenney opened his office three years before the Great Fire. A talented engineer and architect, he pioneered new techniques for building early iron-skeleton buildings in Chicago's unstable and sandy soil. The talented and young Daniel Burnham, Louis Sullivan, William Holabird, and Martin Roche all worked in Jenney's office before starting their own influential practices.

For the Leiter Company department store, Jenney used eight-story granite piers to create nine bays on the block-long State Street facade. The windows were developed in rhythmic compositions split alternately by single, double, and triple stone columns. Every window is double hung, although Jenney varied their sizes across the elevation. Lower floors received larger numbers of smaller units. Upper floors received correspondingly smaller numbers of much larger windows. These variations are strictly compositional and allude to earlier methods of placing windows in load-bearing masonry facades—where larger openings were only possible at upper floors.

Although not yet an all-glass facade, Jenney's Second Leiter Building clearly demonstrates that iron framing created the possibility. The overall effect is strong and dignified, with the interplay of glass and stone piers reminiscent of Gothic cathedrals—a startling development for a strictly commercial structure. The shorter facades on Van Buren and Congress maintain the same expression, although the alley elevation is clad in brick—an aesthetic similar to warehouses and mills developed earlier in the nineteenth century.

A generation older than his employees who reshaped Chicago in the last two decades of the nineteenth century, Jenney had great influence over the development of the new tall buildings. The Second Leiter Building is his sophisticated mix of historical precedent and a rational approach, resolving old forms with the new technologies that were available.

The Monadnock

Burnham & Root, 1891
53 West Jackson Boulevard

The Monadnock is a paradoxical design. Its two-hundred-foot-tall load-bearing masonry walls stretched this ages-old building technology to its uppermost limits. But despite the conservative structure, its bold and spare forms point toward the mid-twentieth century's taste for minimalism and the late twentieth century's infatuation with architectural drama.

The building was built entirely of a dark brown brick. Its base is six-feet thick with deeply set storefronts under heavy lintels. Above the first floor, the wall sweeps inward, while projecting bays create a vertical rhythm across the building's facades. Devoid of ornament in any traditional sense, Root uses massing alone to create a clearly discernable base, middle, and top, as if the entire building was molded from a single piece of dark clay.

The tower is narrow at its north entrance face on Jackson Boulevard, with long facades along its east and west sides. A later addition designed in a more conventional steel frame sits to the south end of the block. Root's only sharp angles in the facade come at the north corners of the building. But as the tower rises, these corners subtly soften as they reach toward the sky. At the building's summit, the tall brick wall flares outward—an inversion of the sweep at the base.

The Monadnock's design was slow in developing, taking most of the second half of the 1880s. Construction was not completed until shortly after John Wellborn Root's untimely death. Its use of traditional load-bearing technology, admired by early critics and fellow architects, has often obscured the radical nature of its outward form.

FOR RENT
OFFICES
APPLY
Aldis, Aldis & Northcott
ON THE PREMISES

13697

Marquette Building

Holabird & Roche, 1893–95
140 South Dearborn Street

The Marquette Building is the best synthesized design of late-nineteenth-century Chicago architecture. Holabird & Roche balanced innovation and tradition to present something that was new, understandable, and comfortable.

The building rises from the sidewalk in a sheer vertical wall to a broad cornice atop the seventeen-story building. Its C-shaped plan conceals a light court open to the alley behind. The facade is classically organized as a base, shaft, and capital to imbue it with a traditional sense of solidity and composition. But the monochromatic brown terra cotta and brick skin hangs from a metal-framed structure. Ornamented decorative features, cast in terra cotta to emulate traditional masonry, are contained within the grid's rigid confines. End bays with richly abstracted geometric articulation frame the street facades and emphasize the building's vertical nature.

"Chicago windows" provide optimal interior daylighting and natural ventilation to the offices. This local innovation combines a large, fixed-glass pane bracketed by two operable windows. The inherent horizontality of the Chicago window creates a subtle tension between each opening and the facade's generally vertical emphasis.

The entrance is based on traditional Ionic pilasters, although its use of a center pilaster is decidedly unorthodox. The hexagonal double-height lobby is equally eccentric as it is centered on a single column. An elaborate mosaic cycle relates the tale of Marquette's journeys.

The Marquette was praised when completed for its combination of businesslike economy and artistic embellishment. Despite its aesthetic success, the building has not survived without change. The westernmost bay along Adams was added in 1905. The cornice was removed in 1950. It was restored in 2003 atop the seventeenth floor.

Reliance Building

Burnham & Root, 1891–95
32 North State Street

The Reliance Building is considered the forefather of the twentieth-century steel and glass skyscraper, due to the unprecedented glassiness of its facades. But to define it solely through the prism of later structures renders a disservice to the marvelous Gothic-inspired structure.

John Root prepared the initial designs for the structure, and the ornamental iron and red Scotch granite of the first two floors still bear his imprint. Following Root's untimely death in 1891, Charles

Atwood completed the steel-framed, fifteen-story, two-hundred-food-tall building. He utilized shallow bays—one along State and two facing Washington—to increase the building's footprint and gain views up and down the streets. Terra cotta spandrels between floors are richly decorated with Gothic motifs, building on the slender vertical columns that separate the windows. There is a rhythmic pattern to the facade, reminiscent of the Monadnock, but the Reliance's sweep of glass and the shiny terra cotta finish give it a much brighter personality than the somber elegance of the earlier design. The building is capped by an extraordinarily thin cornice, another element that looked ahead to a greater lightness in buildings that were to be considered "modern."

Once the design was finished, the building's rapid construction demonstrated the economies inherent in the new steel construction. The framing for the top eight floors was erected in only two weeks. The Reliance Building's white, enameled terra cotta facing was advertised as self-cleaning—an unfortunate overstatement of that new technology's advantages. It was long encrusted in soot and dirt, and a 1996 remodeling and cleaning revealed the building's startling fresh aesthetic.

Historians have speculated that the white cladding was consciously chosen by Burnham and Atwood to emulate their successful planning of the White City at the World's Columbian Exposition of 1893.

RELIANCE - BLD.

Lapp & Flershe

WM T. BARNUM

Chicago Cultural Center

Shepley, Rutan & Coolidge, 1891–97
78 East Washington Street

The architectural motifs of ancient Greece and Rome were used for public buildings in America from the earliest colonial settlements, but the success of the 1893 World's Columbian Exposition in Jackson Park set off a building boom in the classical style for civic and cultural buildings across the nation. Today's Chicago Cultural Center was initially built for dual purposes. It was the city's central library and a monument dedicated to the Civil War's Grand Army of the Republic (GAR).

The unified facade along Michigan Avenue faces Grant Park and gives the impression of a single institution designed according to the classical precepts of the École des Beaux Arts in Paris. Sheathed entirely in Bedford limestone, a full-story base sits below double-height arches. The two upper floors are articulated by Ionic columns supporting a deep and highly decorated cornice. The contrasting articulation of the entrances on the north and south faces of the building express the two different identities.

The library was accessed via an arched entrance on Washington. Mosaic-lined stairs lead to Preston Bradley Hall—a reading room capped by a thirty-eight-foot-diameter Tiffany stained-glass dome. The GAR portion of the building is entered via a Greek portico on Randolph. A semicircular stair leads to a suite of public rooms that commemorate Civil War battles. The GAR Rotunda features a stained-glass dome above a glass-block floor.

Since 1977 the building has housed cultural entities that include galleries, an auditorium, and the city's office of cultural affairs. All library functions eventually moved to the Harold Washington Library Center in 1991.

The building's architects, Shepley, Rutan and Coolidge, were the Boston-based successor to the office of H. H. Richardson. The same designers built the Michigan Avenue building for the Art Institute of Chicago.

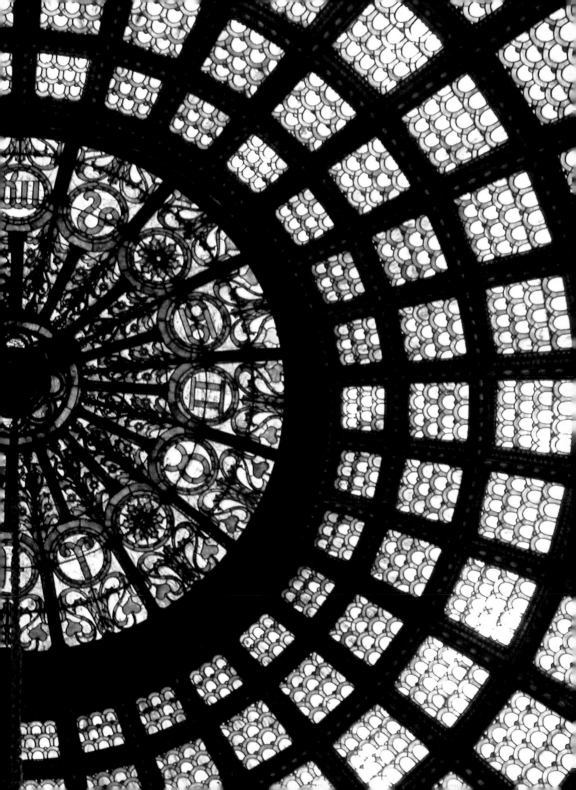

Carson Pirie Scott & Co.
originally **Schlesinger & Mayer**

Louis H. Sullivan, 1899, 1902–03
1 South State Street

Designed for merchandisers Leopold Schlesinger and David Mayer, Louis Sullivan's State Street department store virtually explodes with the architect's exuberant ornamentation. Even today, Sullivan's ornament remains fresh and new. It is his highly original expression of a Whitmanesque intertwining of natural forms and American democracy.

Sullivan designed three portions of the existing structure. A three-bay-wide, nine-story-tall portion was built on Madison Street in 1899. A twelve-story-tall addition was finished four years later—three additional bays on Madison and another three along State linked by the great circular corner that celebrates the importance of State and Madison as the zero point in

Chicago's street numbering system. Sullivan subsequently added four more bays along State. The remainder was added by D. H. Burnham & Company, following Sullivan's design in most details. By the time Sullivan's first addition was completed, the store had been sold to Carson Pirie Scott & Co., who remained custodians of the landmark design throughout the twentieth century.

The most intense ornament occurs on the lowest two floors of the building, where Sullivan created a cast-iron tracery dramatically surrounding the sidewalk windows. It is possible to pick out the monograms of S&M and LHS—the original proprietors and the architect—lurking in the foliage. The middle floors are clad in white terra cotta with Chicago windows deeply set into the facade. The surrounding trim is richly decorated in Sullivan's abstract, geometric ornamentation. The top floor is capped with a deep cornice set above a loggia to create an even greater sense of depth to the facade.

Although Sullivan designed major projects in Chicago and New York at the same time as the Schlesinger & Mayer, it would be his last significant project in Chicago. Within a decade, recurring bouts of alcoholism—not to mention an irascible and artistic temperament—led to greatly diminished commissions in the last years of his life.

Macy's State Street

originally **Marshall Field & Co.**

D. H. Burnham & Co., 1902, 1907
111 North State Street

Daniel Burnham began his work for Marshall Field in 1892, when his firm produced a rusticated structure on the corner of Wabash and Washington for the famed retailer. Burnham's most enduring design for Field, however, was produced to the west of his earlier building between 1902 and 1907.

Although the central entrance and north half of the structure were built five years before the south portion, the completed building is a single composition—a 385-foot-long, twelve-story, urbane structure for retailing that fills the block between Randolph and Washington streets. The limestone facades are simple in detail with a two-story articulated base and a stringcourse that defines an attic above the tenth floor. All openings, except the ground-floor displays, are Chicago windows.

While Louis Sullivan gave Carson Pirie Scott an exciting facade with stoic interiors of little note two blocks south, Burnham did the opposite for the competing Marshall Field. His sober exterior hides dramatic interiors that enliven the store to the present day. Two atriums punctuate the interior design. A five-story space on the south half of the building culminates in a barrel vault finished with a Tiffany mosaic. On the north half, a space ringed with Corinthian columns rises the full height of the building to a skylight.

The 1893 World's Columbian Exposition affected no Chicago architect more dramatically than its principal planner, Daniel Burnham. He became a strong advocate for classical design, culminating in the 1909 *Plan of Chicago* that effects planning in the city to the present day. Unlike his firm's earlier, more experimental work such as the Monadnock and the Reliance, Marshall Field & Co. building, now Macy's State Street, gracefully expresses the conservative tendencies of his later work.

47

Robie House

Frank Lloyd Wright, 1909
5757 South Woodlawn Avenue

The Robie House's striking silhouette is based on its strong horizontal lines that still challenge the University of Chicago's vertically oriented Gothic structures across the street. Long considered one of the most important of Wright's Prairie School works, its urban site is unusual. Most of Wright's residential projects from this period in his career are in suburban locales such as nearby Oak Park. Wright adds spatial drama to the groundbreaking formal work of his predecessors—chiefly Louis Sullivan and H. H. Richardson—in his search for a new, authentically American architecture.

A shallow-sloped roof covers the second-floor rooms and boldly cantilevers over the outdoor terraces to the edge of the sidewalk. Tucked under this broad canopy are the house's principal spaces—the living and dining rooms—separated by Wright's signature central fireplace. These two rooms share a continuous row of art-glass doors and windows that visually extend these spaces out of doors to the west, south, and east.

Wright creates this sense of visual openness on such an exposed corner lot in the city by carefully tucking other necessary spaces into discrete locations. The entrance is hidden down a narrow path behind the main mass, its location indicating the house's privacy. The first floor is slightly below the level of the sidewalk, and both the family room and an adjacent outdoor play area are hidden behind imposing Roman brick walls. The bedrooms are located on a small third floor that rises above the main roof. The garage is behind the house within a private court. Space for three cars is part of an interlocking volume set back from the street that contains servants' quarters, kitchen, and laundry, and doesn't disrupt the carefully planned flow of the main house's spaces.

The Robie House balances two conflicting ideas—an intense sense of privacy inherent in Wright's notion of individualism and an expansive development of space that seeks to embrace the American continent to the horizon.

Wrigley Building

Graham Anderson Probst & White, 1919–24
400–410 North Michigan Avenue

Chicago's Graham Anderson Probst & White was a bit tardy when it adapted La Giralda—the 318-foot-tall, sixteenth-century tower of Seville's Cathedral—as its signature stroke for the Wrigley Building. This model was already a popular choice among American architects who sought historical examples to inform their new skyscraper designs, including Stanford White's Madison Square Garden (1891, 323 feet tall) in New York and the Ferry Building (1898, 240 feet tall) in San Francisco. But the Wrigley outdid all others (including the original) with its 438-foot-tall version of the Spanish design with Moorish overtones. Graham's designers followed the original profile closely but employed French Renaissance motifs for the building's many decorative flourishes.

The Wrigley Building was the first tall office building north of the Chicago River on Michigan Avenue. It is actually two buildings—the main block of twenty-seven stories and an eighteen-story north addition—joined by a street-level arcade and a bridge at the fourteenth floor. Michigan Avenue and the Chicago River shift within the city's grid in front of the Wrigley Building, which creates an unusual trapezoidal site. This anomaly creates memorable views of the building from both the east and the south.

The original terra cotta cladding varied from light gray to titanium white as it rose on the building, but this subtlety has been lost due to weathering. Over time, plastic facsimiles cast in a uniform cream hue have replaced many of the facade's original ornaments. The building's light coloration is itself unusual for Chicago. Coupled with its prominent location, extensive nighttime illumination, and a four-sided clock that is readable from many locales downtown, the Wrigley Building has been a landmark since its opening.

The Wrigley Building was the tallest building in the city for the first two years of its existence. It remains the international headquarters for the chewing gum company that commissioned the design.

Tribune Tower

Howells & Hood, 1923–25
435 North Michigan Avenue

To celebrate the seventy-fifth anniversary of the *Chicago Tribune* in 1922, publisher Robert R. McCormick and editor Joseph M. Patterson held an international architectural competition to immodestly "erect the most beautiful and distinctive office building in the world." New York architects John Mead Howells and Raymond M. Hood's soaring, steel-framed, limestone-clad Gothic design was chosen the winner of 263 entries from twenty-three countries. It forms part of an important urban ensemble that spans Michigan Avenue and the Chicago River, with the Wrigley Building to its west, the London Guarantee Building south of the river, and 333 North Michigan Avenue, also south of the river.

The thirty-four-story, 463-foot-tall tower is an amalgamation of both English and French Gothic precedents. It culminates in an octagonal spire laced with layers of Gothic tracery and supported by eight large flying buttresses. The buttresses spring from primary piers that start at the base of the building and divide each facade into smaller, vertically oriented slots of windows and spandrels. Despite the external drama, much of the space at the top of the tower is dedicated to the prosaic requirements of mechanical equipment. The few offices above the twenty-fifth floor are small and cramped. An open-air observatory on the twenty-fifth floor operated until the 1950s. Below the spire, a more conventional rectangular floor plan is achieved by the addition of a bustle along the east side of the tower.

The building is entered through a tall stone arch decorated with carvings of characters from *Aesop's Fables*, not to mention some metaphorical representations of the building's creators—McCormick, Patterson, Howells, and Hood. The soaring main lobby is most expressive of the churchlike qualities implicit in the tower's forms. Dubbed the Hall of Inscriptions, it has chiseled historical quotations that exhort passing writers and editors in their practice of a free press.

Although the building remains a perennial favorite of both locals and visitors, the architectural cognoscenti still lament Eliel Saarinen's more progressive design, which received second place in the competition.

Carl Street Studios

also known as **151 West Burton**

Sol Kogen, Edgar Miller, and others, 1927
155 West Burton Place

Although Chicago's architecture isn't without its moments of whimsy and caprice, the utterly ad hoc, to-the-limit, crockery-shattering forms of the Carl Street Studios are hardly typical. Sol Kogen and Edgar Miller, an architect and an artist respectively, renovated a series of adjacent Victorian structures into an interconnected gated community with eccentric apartments and a variety of shared outdoor courtyard and rooftop spaces.

Native Chicagoan Kogen was inspired by a short stay on the Left Bank of Paris to develop the property as artists' studios, eventually home to the Old Town Artists Colony. Documentation for the renovation is sparse, but it is known that Kogen and Miller collaborated for about ten years. Attribution of individual elements to either designer is often impossible, and much design work was apparently conducted on the spot. It is hard to tell where the existing buildings end and the Kogen/Miller interventions begin. Found materials and objects scavenged from construction sites and junkyards were incorporated, usually in demonstrably odd ways. Broken ceramics, roofing tiles, and stone shards appear throughout—as decorative features and as walls and floors.

The spatial development of the buildings was equally unusual, with many units spanning two or even three floors. Stairs are often adventurously narrow, winding constructions with treacherously uneven steps. Stained art glass is employed in large, usually tall windows carved from the existing masonry walls. These often denote the location of multi-level units. A half-timbered bay suspended over a side yard could have been salvaged from Elizabethan England. A curved balcony near the main entry to the complex might have been lifted from Le Corbusier's contemporaneous work in Paris (something Kogen would have known from his stay there), except that its railing is rendered in a haphazard manner from metal that likely had an earlier, humbler life somewhere else.

As late as the 1980s, the then-elderly Edgar Miller returned to the complex and executed new murals for several apartments.

Chicago Board of Trade

Holabird & Root, 1930
141 West Jackson Boulevard

The Chicago Board of Trade Building's distinctive silhouette has defined the city's financial district since 1885, when it moved to its prime position at the foot of LaSalle Street. Holabird & Root's 609-foot, forty-five-story structure replaced a building by W. W. Boyington, architect of the Chicago Water Tower.

Designed in the fashionable art deco style, the Board of Trade Building is a sculptural tour de force, its every line and decorative detail pointing skyward. Three distinct floor plates culminate in a pyramidal roof topped by a thirty-one-foot statue of Ceres, the Roman goddess of grains. The first eight floors fill the entire site and contain the lobby and old trading rooms. Fifty-seven-foot-tall windows facing Lasalle Street indicate the location of the original trading floor and orient the potentially boxy base upward. Floors nine through twenty-three are U-shaped. Well suited for the offices of larger trading firms, the shape echoes the canyonlike effect of LaSalle Street and sets the stage for the building's culmination. The upper twenty-two floors are within a notched tower that accommodates smaller brokers' offices while punctuating the building and LaSalle Street.

The building's three-story lobby is the city's premier art deco interior—a collage of stone, metal, and light that evokes the pulsing urbanity of its Jazz Age origins. Sculpted piers separated by billowing clouds of stone support what was reputed to be the world's largest light fixture across the ceiling.

Trading activities moved to a Helmut Jahn–designed annex structure to the south in 1982. A further addition to the east was completed in 1997. An observation deck originally sat at the base of the roof and provided panoramic views of the city from the 1930s through the 1970s. Of all Chicago's buildings, only the Sears Tower has topped the city's skyline longer than the Chicago Board of Trade Building.

Merchandise Mart

Graham Anderson Probst & White, 1927–31
222 Merchandise Mart Plaza

Built for Marshall Field & Company, this massive art deco structure consolidated more than a dozen wholesale goods facilities operated by the department store, and provided a central facility for several hundred smaller firms. The eighteen-story building contains four million square feet and was the largest building in the world when it was completed.

Although it fills two entire city blocks, the building's immense facades were mitigated by establishing a rhythm of vertical limestone piers. Eight-sided towers anchor each of the building's corners. A rectangular tower with a pyramidal roof marks the center of the south facade and indicates the main entrance. Two subtle setbacks occur at the uppermost levels of the building to break some of the monotony without unduly sacrificing floor area.

The public front of the building is oriented toward the river, where it faced the recently completed double-decked Wacker Drive on the opposite bank. A two-story base of public display windows, surrounded with shallow bronze ornamentation line the south, east, and west faces. An elegant double-height limestone lobby connects the south entrance to an east-to-west interior pedestrian street. This handsomely finished passageway links the multitude of passenger elevators required by the massive building. Services for the building's tenants and visitors line the interiors on the lowest two floors. A two-block-long loading dock once spanned the rear of the building.

The upper floors were completed as raw spaces of five acres each, marked only by a nineteen-and-a-half-foot grid of concrete columns. Only two small lightwells serve these interiors. All interior spaces were outfitted with artificial ventilation and lighting—considered most conducive to showing various goods in as controlled an environment as possible.

The building opened six months after the onset of the Depression and rendered H. H. Richardson's Marshall Field Wholesale Store obsolete. That influential structure was demolished within the year. In 1943 the Pentagon supplanted the Mart as the world's largest building. The Mart was sold two years later to Joseph P. Kennedy, former ambassador and father of the future president.

University Building

Keck & Keck, 1937

5551 South University Avenue

Brothers George Fred and William Keck were innovators responsible for two important designs at Chicago's 1933 Century of Progress Exposition—the House of Tomorrow and the Crystal House. During the Depression years, their firm of Keck & Keck produced fine small houses in the modern style that had been codified by the Museum of Modern Art *International Architecture* exhibition in 1932.

The University Building is a variation of the standard Chicago three-flat—a stack of three apartments, each occupying a single floor. The thirty-foot-wide structure is located on a double-width lot, and its load-bearing masonry walls support steel joists and concrete decking. Technically the structure is a three-story building, as the designers located only the three-car garage, a laundry room, and other nonliving service spaces on the ground level—rendering it an above-ground basement for zoning purposes.

The front facade epitomizes the most up-to-date approach of the time, stressing clean lines with no ornamentation. The three-bay rhythm is derived from the garage doors that face the street, since there is no back alley. Red-orange brick blends with the neighboring structures. The windows stress the two outermost bays and read as dark vertical slots against the plain brick walls. External aluminum Venetian blinds are a key functional and aesthetic feature. Originally adjustable, they were eventually replaced with fixed units due to maintenance problems. The windows open inward.

The apartments are entered from either side, directly off a central stairwell. This arrangement allowed the possibility of subdividing the second- and third-floor apartments into additional units. Each apartment of the cooperative building was specifically designed for its owner. The second floor originally contained a four-bedroom unit for the Gottschalks—a University of Chicago professor and his family. The third-floor apartment was a three-bedroom unit for George Fred Keck, who created an outdoor living area in the rear of the building. William Keck and his wife owned the top-floor unit—which was only half the size of the Gottschalks'—with a very large outdoor living space at the rear.

Even today, the University Building's clean lines and well-proportioned windows and walls make it seem very contemporary.

Myron Bachman House

Bruce Goff, 1948
1244 West Carmen Avenue

Bruce Goff was one of architecture's true eccentrics. His exuberant designs, which often featured unorthodox geometries and whirling vortices, owe a debt to his early-career heroes, Louis Sullivan and Frank Lloyd Wright. While seldom thought of as a Chicago architect, he practiced for nearly a decade in the city before moving in 1946 to teach at the University of Oklahoma at Norman, where he built his best-known works. The Myron Bachman House is one of only two projects in the Chicago area that he designed after leaving the city.

The project is an addition and renovation of an 1889 wood-frame house. Goff's design created new living spaces and a new studio for Myron Bachman, a recording engineer.

Goff served in the Navy as a Seabee during World War II, and his military experience with Quonset hut technology is obvious in the Bachman addition's most prominent material. Goff re-roofed the original house in corrugated metal and extended the gable front into a diamond-shaped motif that evokes the space age—a decade before Sputnik.

He extended the house to the sidewalk on the ground floor, wrapping it in a slightly askew brick wall topped in a corrugated metal fascia. Throughout his career, Goff was a master of using unusual building materials, famously incorporating coal and crystals into his work. His idiosyncratic work remains startling today, especially on this rather traditional residential Uptown block.

860–880 North Lake Shore Drive

Ludwig Mies van der Rohe, 1949–51
860–880 North Lake Shore Drive

This pair of twenty-six-story, 270-foot-tall black steel and glass towers seems unexceptional today, but they spawned clones that defined the look of global architecture for the next half century. Before 860–880, Chicago's lakefront residential apartment buildings were almost exclusively masonry clad and filled their pricey building lots to the edges. Mies set two identical rectangular towers perpendicular to each other on the trapezoidal block-long site. Each is divided into three-by-five bays of twenty-one feet square. A two-story base set back from the face of the structures reveals the bay system while creating a colonnade that provides cover for residents entering the buildings.

Vertical window mullions run the height of the towers, and their I-beam shape reflects the actual structural frame that is hidden beneath fireproof covering. Mies's use of these standard shapes in a manner that was clearly ornamental rather than structural caused some consternation among his acolytes. Well known for his statement that "Less is more," the master clearly demonstrated here that aesthetics sometimes warrant the use of a little more.

Mies conceived the original apartments with open-plan configurations. But while progressive developer Herbert Greenwald was willing to gamble on a steel and glass exterior, he insisted on more conventional apartments. In fact, many units that have been renovated by the architects and design buffs who inhabit the buildings are truer in spirit to the architect's original concept than their initial layouts. Greenwald kept an apartment available for Mies, but the architect never moved from the traditional masonry apartment building where he dwelled for all of his years in Chicago.

Despite its great design influence, 860–880 remains something of an anomaly in Chicago for its steel-frame structure. The vast majority of apartment buildings in the city—regardless of exterior cladding—are actually concrete-frame buildings. And most of the buildings that Mies's design spawned were actually office buildings.

Crown Hall

Ludwig Mies van der Rohe, 1956
3360 South State Street

Mies van der Rohe designed several dozen buildings for the South Side Illinois Institute of Technology, where he was campus planner and director of the School of Architecture. Most of these structures employ a brick and glass infill system within an exposed steel frame. Mies deviated from this norm when he conceived Crown Hall as home for the architecture school. He created a single eighteen-foot-tall space under a 120-by-220-foot structure enclosed entirely in glass. It is sometimes facetiously regarded as the last single-room schoolhouse built in America.

Four six-foot-deep steel plate girders support the structure's roof from above, so that the ceiling is a single floating plane only twice interrupted by mechanical chases. Like a classical temple, the building's main floor is set six feet above the adjacent lawn, which allows for clerestory windows to the basement spaces. Significantly, Crown Hall was the first large-scale, clear-span structure that Mies constructed.

The building's skin is divided into two levels of glass. An eight-foot band of translucent glazing around the floor creates a soft, natural light that is meant to focus students' attention away from activities external to the building. A clear glass upper band dematerializes the skin and gives generous views of the ever-changing sky and the swaying branches of nearby trees.

Crown Hall was such a successful icon of modern architecture that it served as the foil for Chicago architect Stanley Tigerman's 1978 satirical collage titled *The Titanic* (see pages 78–79). At the moment in history when architects began to question the relevancy of Mies's work, it depicted Crown Hall slipping beneath the waves of Lake Michigan to a watery grave.

30 West Monroe
originally **Inland Steel Building**

Skidmore Owings & Merrill, 1958
30 West Monroe Street

Even when glass is the predominant exterior material, most of Chicago's metal-framed skyscrapers have dark, even somber, structures. But the Inland Steel Building, now formally recognized as 30 West Monroe, glistens and shimmers in the sunlight due to its bright, innovative stainless steel exterior cladding. It still radiates the optimism appropriate to its status as the first new office structure within the Loop to be completed in the quarter century after the onset of the Depression.

The building is split into two distinct structures: a nineteen-story, 250-foot-tall glass-sheathed office structure and a twenty-five-story, 330-foot-tall window-less stainless steel service tower. Skidmore Owings & Merrill (SOM) partner Walter Netsch initiated the concept. Bruce Graham, working for the first time with structural engineer Fazlur Khan, developed the final building details.

Seven pairs of external structural columns support sixty-foot girders from the east and west sides of the office block. Since elevators, fire stairs, and bathrooms are relegated to the service tower, the resulting office floors, of 10,300 square feet each, have no interior obstructions. The north and south ends of the tower are cantilevered twenty feet and provide glassy corner offices that hover in the air.

Entry is via a two-story lobby under the main building block's cantilever facing Monroe Street. A reflecting pool and sculpture animate the elegant space that leads to the service tower and its elevators.

For many years, SOM maintained their offices within the building. Today, it is partially owned by Frank Gehry and is home to a number of architectural firms that value the building's iconic Mid-Century Modern aesthetic and find the open floor plans conducive to studio environments.

Marina City

Bertrand Goldberg Associates, 1962–64
300 North State Street

Bertrand Goldberg's concept for Marina City was revolutionary in its day. It was a place to live, work, and play within a single downtown complex, not to mention that its dual concrete towers looked like little else that had ever been built before. Round rather than rectangular, sculptural rather than stoic, Marina City's twin sixty-five-story residential towers are the anti-Mies. The complex also includes a sixteen-story commercial/office building (now a hotel), a saddle-backed theater structure (now an entertainment facility), and other amenities such as a bowling alley and a restaurant.

The upper forty floors of each tower contain a total of 896 apartments. Each apartment has its own semicircular balcony. The lower levels are an exposed helical ramped parking structure. The circular towers emanate from a concrete core that carries much of the weight of each tower. Each floor is subdivided into sixteen equal portions and resembles a flower petal in plan. Apartments are devoid of parallel walls, an oddity that was never an impediment to its marketability. All units were rented upon completion. Later converted to a condominium, the building has never had a problem with occupancy.

Another innovation was Goldberg's recognition of the Chicago River as an amenity. The lowest level of the complex is at water level. The river moorings make the development's name more than just a marketer's ploy.

Due to evolving uses, Marina City no longer functions as a self-contained "city within a city." But the success of Chicago's downtown residential living today owes a debt to this pioneering complex.

Richard J. Daley Center
originally **Chicago Civic Center**

Chicago Civic Center Architects
(C. F. Murphy & Associates, with Skidmore Owings &
Merrill and Loebl Schlossman & Bennett), 1965
55 West Randolph Street

Now named for the mayor who was its patron, this brawny tower and the simple plaza that fronts it was originally called the Chicago Civic Center. Daniel Burnham first proposed the name for an enormous public square west of the Loop that was the focal point of his celebrated 1909 Plan of Chicago. C. F. Murphy designer Jacques Brownson developed the essentials of the design while collaborating with three of Chicago's largest architectural firms.

The 648-foot-tall, thirty-one-story structure is located at the north side of the site to capture direct sunlight from the south. The building contains spaces for Cook County, the State of Illinois, and the City of Chicago, but its 120 courtrooms were the most important feature in the program. Providing for their flexible arrangement drove the building's design. These assembly spaces each required taller ceilings and more extensive mechanical systems than a standard office building.

Brownson devised a structure supported by only sixteen cruciform columns with bays of extraordinarily long spans—each segment is eighty-seven feet long by forty-eight feet wide. The finished ceilings are twelve feet high in the courtrooms, and floor-to-floor heights are eighteen feet. On the facade, the columns step back as they rise, and the exposed six-feet-deep girders express a monumentality akin to the giant order columns of the City Hall/County Building across the street. The exterior steel is Cor-Ten—an innovative, self-weathering material that has acquired an elegant red patina since the building's completion.

The fifty-foot-tall sculpture (shown on following pages) in the plaza was designed by Pablo Picasso and engineered by Skidmore Owings & Merrill in the same Cor-Ten material that supports the building. Picasso worked solely in models (the original is in the Art Institute of Chicago) and never actually saw the space.

John Hancock Center

Skidmore Owings & Merrill, 1965–69
875 North Michigan Avenue

innovative, trussed tube structural system conceived by engineer Fazlur Khan, who at the time was just thirty-five years old.

The mixed-use building comprises some 2.8 million square feet of space and includes shopping in a below-grade plaza, parking (accessed by a spiral concrete ramp), offices, and apartments, with a restaurant and observation deck at the top. The structure's unusual sloped form has a dual purpose. It helps stabilize the building in the wind, but just as important, it accommodates the different floor plate requirements of the building's many uses. Offices fill the lower, larger floors, while apartments—whose living spaces require natural ventilation and cannot be located as far from the exterior wall—occupy the upper levels. The exterior walls of the tower slope inward as its rectangular plan ranges from 165 by 265 feet at its base to 100 by 160 feet at the roof. The X-bracing significantly reduced the quantity of steel necessary to achieve such a great height.

Topping out at 1,127 feet, the John Hancock Center's boldly expressive diagonal bracing gives it a strong character that even larger buildings lack. Its distinctive, yet simple form is an icon of Chicago. No child's sketch of the city's skyline is complete without its slightly canted sides and gigantic X-bracing. The architectural design is attributed to Skidmore Owings & Merrill's Bruce Graham, but the building's look is expressive of the

When Hancock was completed in 1969, it was the tallest building in Chicago, and only New York's Empire State Building soared higher. A stark reminder of the difficulties of building tall, the design and construction of the building took almost five years, including a shutdown of more than six months, when uneven settlement of the building's foundations threatened catastrophic structural failure.

er Place

McCormick Place

C. F. Murphy & Associates, 1967–71
2301 South Lake Shore Drive

Although designed by Gene Summers, McCormick Place is derivative of a long-span convention center proposed by Mies van der Rohe for a nearby site on the South Side. Summers worked for Mies for the better part of two decades and had only recently established his own small office when an earlier version of McCormick Place was destroyed by fire. The firm C. F. Murphy was retained for the job and hired Summers specifically to design the new structure.

C. F. Murphy unsuccessfully attempted to involve Mies in the project, but his employee of two weeks—new Illinois Institute of Technology alumnus Helmut Jahn—used the opportunity as a springboard for much future success.

When completed, the building encompassed 522,000 square feet of exhibition space, including 250,000 square feet in a single, glass-enclosed room atop a brick-clad podium. Large cruciform columns support a two-way system of trusses that

span 150 feet. An imposing seventy-five-foot cantilever shelters exterior spaces.

Many changes have been made to the complex since its completion, and newer structures now sprawl many blocks to the west. The most significant modification to the 1971 building was the inclusion of the Twenty-Second Street right of way within the interior of the exhibition hall. When the building first opened, it was possible to drive through it to the lakeside edge of the complex's platform. North of

Twenty-Second Street was exhibition space; south of the opening was the Arie Crown Theater.

The complex is named for longtime *Chicago Tribune* publisher Robert R. McCormick, whose support for a permanent exposition space in the city was crucial to its ultimate realization. The building's lakefront location has always been considered a problematic usurpation of public space for decidedly mercantile purposes.

Federal Center

Ludwig Mies van der Rohe, 1959–74
219 South Dearborn Street

Planned over a five-year period, the Federal Center was not completed until after Mies's 1969 death. The complex comprises three asymmetrically positioned structures on a block-and-a-half, 4.6-acre site that straddles Dearborn Street. A thirty-story courthouse east of Dearborn and a forty-five-story office building to the south along Jackson frame the plaza that contains a single-story post office.

Mies's rigorous geometries are apparent everywhere in the complex. The courthouse's facade is very nearly square, the office building's height is twice its width, and the post office is 197 feet square, divided into nine equal bays. Each building's sober black and gray exterior expression follows the steel mullion and glass model that Mies pioneered at 860–880 North Lake Shore Drive. The architect's insistence on apparent order required some camouflage. The upper floors of the courthouse contain double-height spaces, but they are hidden behind Mies's relentlessly regularized window pattern.

The plaza is paved with granite meticulously set in the same planning module as the window mullions. There is not a single joint that can't be traced across the breadth of the complex and up and down each of the facades, a conceptual integration of the buildings that is unusual in its rigor. Granite security bollards have been added along the streets in recent years.

While they maintain the rich material that Mies employed, they unfortunately compromise the unifying effect that he achieved.

The complex's layout is not without fault. Mies's positioning of the tallest structure along its southern edge shrouds the space in shadow most of the day. He considered other configurations but apparently chose this one to enhance the relationship with the Marquette Building north of the plaza.

The curving forms and bright red paint of Alexander Calder's sculpture offer an exuberant counterpoint to Mies's austerely elegant design. The Federal Center closely parallels his contemporaneous designs for the Toronto Dominion Center and Montreal's Westmount Square.

Sears Tower

Skidmore Owings & Merrill, 1968–74
233 Wacker Drive

Sears Tower was the tallest building in the world for more than two decades, a reign surpassed in the twentieth century only by the Empire State Building. Its dark metal form sitting toward the south end of the city's skyline creates a bookend effect with the John Hancock Center to the north. The same design team as Hancock—architect Bruce Graham and engineer Fazlur Khan of Skidmore Owings & Merrill (SOM)—developed the innovative structural system of nine bundled tubes that allows Sears Tower to scrape the sky at 1,450 feet.

The tower is situated on a full city block of three acres and contains over 4.4 million square feet of interior space. A square plan of 225 feet is subdivided into nine structural modules of 75 by 75 feet each. The first fifty floors fill the entire envelope. From the fiftieth through the sixty-sixth floor, two bays at opposing corners were omitted to create an asymmetrical plan. From the sixty-sixth to the ninetieth floor, two additional bays were removed to create a cruciform shape. The final twenty floors comprise only two structural tubes and give the tower an east-west orientation. The effect is similar to the ziggurat type of high-rise design that was popular in New York and other cities during the early years of the skyscraper.

The tower sits on an open plaza on the block bounded by Adams, Jackson, Wacker, and Franklin. For all the daring engineering that went into the building's structural design, SOM's architects struggled with placing an acceptable front door on a facade that is a quarter of a mile tall. Today's main entrance off Wacker is a barrel-vaulted addition designed by SOM in 1984 and since remodeled by Destefano+Partners.

Sears Tower was originally designed to house seven thousand company employees with eventual expansion to the entire structure with thirteen thousand workers. The retailer sold the tower in 1989 and completed its move out of the building in 1995, but the building's iconic status led subsequent owners to retain the name.

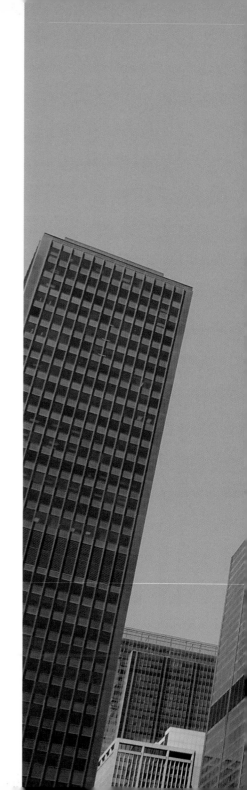

Metropolitan Correctional Facility

Harry Weese & Associates, 1975
71 West Van Buren Street

Chicago's architecture was dominated by rather strait-laced architectural expression after Mies van der Rohe's arrival in1938. During the next four decades, Bertrand Goldberg was one notable exception who sought more evocative solutions; Harry Weese was the other. In his Metropolitan Correctional Facility, Weese grappled with unusual challenges. He created a prison in a downtown location, broke the predominant gridiron pattern with a triangular floor plan, and attempted to provide humane facilities for a most inhumane architectural program.

The facility houses prisoners for short-term stays while they are on trial at the nearby Federal Center. A high-rise solution was chosen because it facilitates the isolation of its occupants. While logical for housing prisoners, it raises interesting philosophical questions about many of Chicago's best-known buildings, which are similarly tall.

The twenty-seven-story tower's triangular floor plan maximizes the building's perimeter to provide more space for windows, while minimizing the length of interior corridors. Inmates inhabit private cells with a five-inch-wide window, based on the maximum allowable spacing between prison bars to prevent escape. The windows are splayed outward to capture as much daylight within these narrow constraints. Weese mitigated the potentially oppressive facades by spacing the windows in a random pattern that dances across the exposed concrete facades. Divided into two programmatic halves, mechanical floors occupy a windowless zone at the middle of the tower. The lower portion houses administration and social service functions. Detention cells are located in the upper half, with a rooftop exercise yard crowning the structure.

The concrete building is a bearing-wall structure, supported on three corner piers at its base. Transfer beams are incorporated into the wall to create a glassy two-story lobby whose openness contrasts with the building above. The concrete was originally exposed, although a 2007 renovation has unfortunately muted the intended raw effect by covering it in paint.

Steel & Glass House

Krueck & Olsen, 1981
1949 North Larrabee Street

The Steel & Glass House was Illinois Institute of Technology–trained Ron Krueck's first architectural commission. The client asked for a house that looked like a factory and that incorporated certain typically suburban conveniences into its urban site. Hence, there is a small parking court, and garage access is from the street rather than the alley. While Mies van der Rohe made his architecture of stock steel shapes using the least possible means ("Less is more," as he is oft quoted), a similar vocabulary of steel pieces accomplished very different ends here. The architects Krueck and Olsen used standard steel shapes in a variety of ways, demonstrating the wide range of expression that is possible within this rarified aesthetic.

In what is essentially a glass house in a densely populated urban neighborhood, the architects created privacy from the street by using opaque surfaces on the garage doors and two different translucent materials—glass block and frosted glass—on the front facade. Steel grating screens ordinary glazing for the entry hall.

The double-width house is organized as three pavilions in a U shape around a courtyard facing south, which provides maximum daylight throughout the structure. A two-story living room runs from the front to the rear of the house and is centered on the courtyard. The front pavilion houses the garage on the first floor with a master bedroom on the second. The rear pavilion has kitchen and dining on the first floor with a terrace and guest room above. A slot of light, topped by a skylight, runs the length of the house and divides the three blocks. This narrow zone is expressed on the front facade with full-height clear glazing.

The interiors are an elaboration of the painterly qualities found on the front facade and reflect the client's and architect's interest in Milan design, circa 1970. The original owner served as the general contractor on the project in order to ensure the level of quality that he desired in construction and finishes.

333 Wacker Drive

Kohn Pedersen Fox, 1979–83
333 Wacker Drive

The arrival of 333 Wacker sent serious repercussions through Chicago's architectural community. For one, the gracefully curving facade—which was a perfect reflection of its location at a bend in the Chicago River—disrupted the predominant rectilinear approach that had been Chicago architects' default solution for generations. Second, the New York–based designers broke what had essentially been a closed-shop system. The building heralded the arrival of top-notch out-of-town architects as major players.

The thirty-six-story structure, clad in green glass that reflects the Chicago River's natural hue, is considerably more nuanced than it first seems. The site is actually triangular, and Kohn Pedersen Fox's designers purposefully chose not to follow the site's outline. The curve does not rise the full height of the building. The top is cut at a forty-five-degree angle, subtly providing the broad curve with a backdrop. Vertical aluminum mullions were tinted to match the glass. Stainless steel half-round mullions were used on the horizontal to give the curtain wall a sense of depth. This is an inversion of the pattern seen in the glass facades pioneered by Mies van der Rohe and his acolytes—in which vertical mullions were emphasized over the horizontal.

The "back" of the building—facing the Loop along Lake and Franklin—also steps back from the corner to give four sides to each of the building's floors. The top floors are faceted to acknowledge the primary city grid and add visual interest. The base of the building is articulated in gray granite and green marble. A double-height lobby with an entire floor devoted to mechanical equipment above raises the first occupied office spaces above the adjacent Elevated train lines.

James R. Thompson Center

originally **State of Illinois Building**

Murphy/Jahn, 1979–85
100 West Randolph Street

The James R. Thompson Center houses the Chicago offices of the State of Illinois within a structure named for the former governor who was its chief patron. Its eccentric shape fills three corners of the block bounded by Clark, LaSalle, Randolph, and Lake—with a broadly sweeping curve that leaves the southeast corner of the site an open plaza. The building's sixteen-story height is comparable to that of City Hall to its south, while the plaza provides a continuous public space with the Richard J. Daley Center.

The central feature is a dramatic, 332-foot-tall, 160-foot-diameter atrium that is a nod to the domed rotundas popular in traditional American civic design. But the architects desired to express the idea of open government through open spaces, a concept that works with some efficiency in the offices that ring the upper floors of the atrium. The architectural details at the lower, public levels of the space are more reminiscent of 1970s hotels and shopping malls, rather than the gravitas of most State Houses. Shops line the ground floor of the rotunda, while a seventy-foot opening in the ground floor brings natural light to the lower-level food court.

The final blow to civic grandeur is the exterior glass skin, multicolored with blue, gray, white, silver, and clear glazing. The colors were patterned over building entrances on LaSalle and Lake streets to appear as keystones that span the full height of the structure. Many Chicagoans felt the garish color scheme recalled the 1950s-era Greyhound Terminal that stood across Clark Street rather than either the Daley Center or the City Hall/County Building.

Tunnels connect the Thompson Center to the adjacent public buildings, as well as to the subway at the lower level and the Elevated at the second floor. Designed by the then-forty-one-year-old Helmut Jahn, the building experienced widely reported teething problems immediately following its opening. For many years afterward, Jahn's principal work was outside Chicago—a situation that only started to change some two decades later.

Harold Washington Library Center

Hammond Beeby Babka, 1991
400 South State Street

The creation of the Harold Washington Library Center is reminiscent of the Tribune Tower—both products of widely publicized architectural competitions. Each displays historically derived designs that have been popular with the general public, yet both still cause consternation among the city's architectural cognoscenti.

Tom Beeby's red brick, granite, and glass composition fills a city block facing William Le Baron Jenney's Second Leiter Building. The library uses traditional design motifs to establish itself as a civic structure.

The building is simple in composition. A two-story battered granite base supports a five-story brick body punctuated by five arches along State Street and three facing Congress and Van Buren. The building is topped by a two-story gabled structure whose glass enclosure poses a radical inversion of the massive walls below. The fourth facade, facing Plymouth Court, has glazing throughout, which allows the building to be read as an elaborate stage set.

Library stacks and reading areas are located behind the tall arched windows on floors three through seven. These floors are organized in an open plan for maximum flexibility, reminiscent of the loft-type spaces of the department stores that were State Street's original focus: the Second Leiter Building, Schlessinger & Meyer, and Marshall Field & Co. The top two floors house administrative offices, specialized collections, galleries, and a skylight-topped Winter Garden that functions as a public gathering place.

The most notable feature of the building's decoration is the oversized acroteria that crown the top of the gables and each of the four corners. Basing it on traditional motifs, the architects and artists supersized the leafy ornamentation and symbolic owls in a decidedly looser, contemporary interpretation. The Harold Washington Library Center is a hybrid design that reflects the conflicting architectural ideas that characterized the late 1980s.

132

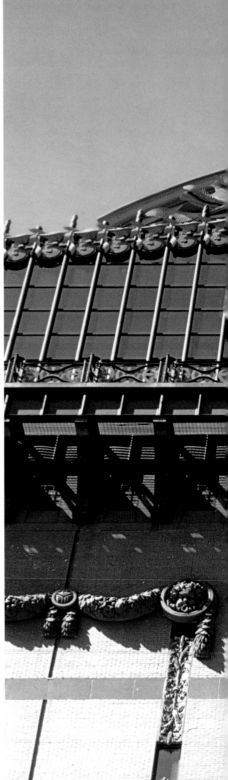

Little Village Academy

Ross Barney+Jankowski, 1996
2620 South Lawndale Avenue

The prominence of the sun in Mexican mythology led Little Village Academy's designers to create a three-and-a-half-story sundial as the building's signature space, recognizing its location in Chicago's most prominent Mexican-American community. The sundial marks the main entrance and is actu-

ally part of a required fire stair. A bright yellow wall splits the multicolored cylinder and extends half a story above the building's roof.

The architects enlivened the school's three-story masonry envelope by dramatically exposing several of the building's significant interior spaces. The building is located on Lawndale Avenue, with protected playgrounds accessible from the first-floor classrooms to the south and a large playing field to the north. A U-shaped corridor wraps first-floor service spaces and a double-height gymnasium on the second floor so that all classrooms and associated teaching spaces face either the street or the playing field. A second-floor science classroom is a featured space, with its rotated translucent walls cantilevered over the building's southeast corner. Similarly, on the third floor, the library anchors the center of the south facade where the story-and-a-half space gathers generous daylight from a clerestory window located above a mural of the school.

Chicago's public schools have a long tradition of serious design, including Prairie School architect and Frank Lloyd Wright contemporary Dwight Perkins. This legacy was eroded during the 1990s by a plethora of banal prototypes built across the city. Little Village Academy restores high design—and community spirit—in a contemporary design worthy of the city's architectural history.

Private Residence

Tadao Ando, 1992–98

With a few notable exceptions, concrete has been used in Chicago for utilitarian and unremarkable buildings. Tadao Ando, the 1995 Pritzker Prize Laureate based in Osaka, Japan, is best known for his poetic buildings constructed of concrete. His single-family residence in Lincoln Park was the architect's first completed building in the United States. It is consistent with the high standards of his work, but it is definitely an unusual presence in a Chicago residential neighborhood.

Located on a seventy-five-foot-wide triple lot, the house is a cloisterlike complex where its occupants can live with nature, sheltered from the city. Privacy is paramount. The front face of the house is protected from the street by a high cast-in-place concrete wall. The large, industrial metal front door evinces no show of neighborliness. Three distinct wings define the house—one for the client, one for his parents, and one for his guests. A reflecting pool of water and gardens separate the wings and give each its privacy from the others. The house was designed around an existing giant poplar tree that is now part of the internal garden. The thick concrete walls sculpt light and shadows within the home's private preserve—an essential theme in all the architect's work.

Ando's high standards for concrete proved a challenge to Chicago's builders. Three contractors were needed over the six-year span it took to construct the relatively small building. More than a few walls were rebuilt several times during construction before the demanding architect found the work acceptable.

Republic Windows & Doors

Booth Hansen Associates, 1998
930 West Evergreen Street

Republic Windows & Doors is a factory that aspires to be a civic building of distinction. Located on Goose Island, the metal-clad plant is part of a Planned Manufacturing District that encourages industrial activity to remain in the city.

The building's steel-framed structure is set on a forty-foot-square grid. Most of the plant, where 700 employees manufacture and sell vinyl windows, comprises a twenty-seven-foot-tall, one-story space. On the building's south edge, three floors of offices stack beneath a splayed roof that rises to fifty feet along the front facade. This face features Republic's corporate entry, monumentalized by architect Larry Booth's one rhetorical flourish: a fifty-foot-tall colonnade that supports a sunscreen, inclined to match the slope of the roof. This potentially gratuitous gesture (it has no practical purpose) imbues the structure with what the architect terms "a civilized presence."

West of the office entrance, raw materials enter through the bays of a loading dock. Fabrication and assembly wind through the factory to the north end of the structure, where another loading dock sends finished products on their way to customers. The exterior of the building is developed in a similarly straightforward way. Each column is a stock-steel I-section that is located outside the building's exterior envelope. Horizontal ribbon windows and corrugated siding slide behind the columns, producing a compelling pattern of light and shadow with simple and inexpensive materials.

Archer Courts

Landon Bone, 2000
2220 South Princeton Avenue

Archer Courts is one of the last remaining vestiges of the public housing projects that the city and state built during the middle decades of the twentieth century. Literally dozens of similarly designed large apartment buildings—with now notorious names such as Stateway Gardens, the Robert Taylor Homes, and Cabrini-Green—have been bulldozed and redeveloped as smaller-scaled neighborhoods.

The 147-unit, seven-story structure built in 1951 was completely renovated. Open-air corridors enclosed in chain-link fencing were a standard feature at Archer Courts and its brethren. Supposedly designed as a common space, these narrow circulation spines were cold in the winter, hot in the summer, and ugly all year round. Landon Bone enclosed the corridors with a standard aluminum curtain wall to make these spaces an internal part of the apartment building. Glazing is both clear and translucent to vary the effect. Adding color to the design is new vinyl flooring in blue with red accents, as well as apartment doors painted in primary hues. At night, interior lighting reflects these colors and gives the new facade a playful appearance where the chain-link galleries once were. Existing brick was cleaned, and the exposed concrete frame was painted to enliven the old building envelopes.

A new single-story structure was added to house community spaces—a large multipurpose room and a wellness center. Mindful of Archer Courts' Chinatown location, the architects incorporated abstracted Chinese features throughout the property, provided areas for Tai Chi, and used Feng Shui principles while planning the new additions.

Archer Courts was one of the first buildings sold by the Chicago Housing Authority to a non-governmental group for redevelopment. Its unique success is a testament to the power of thoughtful design to reinvigorate even the most banal of existing buildings.

Soldier Field

Holabird & Root, 1922–26
Wood+Zapata, with Lohan Caprile Goettsch,
2000–03 renovation
425 East McFetridge Drive

Today's Soldier Field comprises two distinct structures. There is a classical stone-clad shell designed in the 1920s with twin fifty-foot-tall Doric colonnades atop the east and west sides of an elongated Greek amphitheater. Its contemporary interior is a 2003 retrofit designed specifically for the NFL's Chicago Bears. The original stadium seated 120,000 for spectacles that ranged from prizefights to stock car racing to open-air religious gatherings before the Bears made it their home in 1971. The new Soldier Field seats 61,500 in a boldly asymmetrical steel and concrete bowl set within the confines of the original colonnades.

The two structures exist in a dynamic tension. The original is formal, even a bit stuffy—a reminder of the many lakefront buildings designed in the classical style during the decades following the World's Columbian Exposition. The new structure is dynamic and expressive of the dramatic geometries that often mark early-twenty-first-century architecture.

The east grandstand is topped by an enclosed steel and glass structure that protects luxury skyboxes and other high-end amenities in a temperature-controlled environment. The west stands are traditional open seating with the uppermost deck dramatically cantilevering over the old colonnade to gain every inch of space from the existing envelope. The end zones sport soaring scoreboards that hang 90 feet over the stands at the south end and a dazzling 120 feet at the north. Openings between the new east and west structures create visual connections between the stadium and the downtown skyline.

McCormick Tribune Campus Center

OMA/Rem Koolhaas, 2003
3201 South State Street

The Illinois Institute of Technology campus was planned in 1938–41 by Mies van der Rohe and contains the largest collection of buildings designed by the architect. Before 2003 every new structure was highly deferential to the modern master's aesthetic—primarily beige brick, dark gray steel, and clear glass. Pritzker Prize Laureate Rem Koolhaas's McCormick Tribune Campus Center is a determined renegade whose orange and blue glass, black-and-maroon streaked-fascia, and canted roofs crash Mies's refined party like a drunken undergraduate.

The Elevated train line bisects the campus—a residential district to the east and the academic core to the west. Koolhaas ducks his single-story building underneath the existing El structure and acoustically isolates the train's cacophony by wrapping it in a 530-foot stainless steel tube that is the most visually compelling part of his design. Koolhaas knits the two halves of the campus together with a plan of diagonal paths tracing those that college students had long worn across the forlorn field under the El.

The program combines an ambitious amalgam of student-oriented activities and includes a theater, conference room, radio station, coffee bar, convenience store, and bookstore. Casual dining is offered in a lower-level sports bar that is naturally lit through a courtyard, which was created by carving a space next to the foundations of an existing Mies building—the Commons. That structure becomes part of the complex, and its remodeled interior functions as the main campus dining facility. Wide corridors and unconventional spaces allow for happenstance student activities. Ping-pong and billiard tables energize the space directly beneath the stainless steel tube. Computer stations are located in a trough under the roof's lowest point, and quirky graphics abound. Unusual materials and textures are deployed as well. Most ceilings are an unpainted gypsum board with exposed smears of spackle covering the joints and screws.

IIT's unrelentingly serious architecture long gave the campus a rather dour image among prospective students. The McCormick Tribune Campus Center was designed to appeal to a generation raised on the sharp and fleeting graphic indulgences of video and computer games. Koolhaas's finishes intentionally contrast with Mies's materials. It is IIT's twenty-first-century Mies antidote.

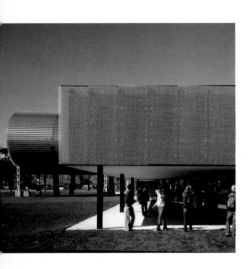

Jay Pritzker Pavilion

Frank O. Gehry & Associates, 2004
Millennium Park

Frank Gehry's dynamic structure forms the architectural centerpiece of the twenty-four-acre lakefront Millennium Park, conceived as a new urban gathering place between 1998 and 2004. The 1989 Pritzker Prize Laureate's trademark stainless steel swirls surround a corrugated metal-clad stage house and create a stunning presence for concertgoers sitting as far as six hundred feet away on the Great Lawn.

The eccentric forms shield various support services for the band shell, including theatrical catwalks that are cantilevered some 70 feet in front of the stage. An enormous curved steel trellis system supports a state-of-the-art sound system suspended above eleven thousand listeners—four thousand in fixed seating adjacent to the stage and seven thousand on the grass. These advanced features are more typical of indoor concert facilities.

Gehry's signature forms, reminiscent of his iconic Guggenheim Museum Bilbao, are best seen from the lawn. It is a highly personalized style developed through a process utilizing traditional 3-D cardboard models and highly advanced computer imaging and engineering. His freely evolved forms are a contemporary interpretation of the ideas that animated Louis Sullivan's evocative interior for the Auditorium Theatre. But Gehry doesn't hide the elaborate structure required to support his exotic creation, engineered in Chicago by Skidmore Owings & Merrill.

He exhibits his design like a stage set, concealing the struts and supports only when the facade is viewed from the preferred location of the audience.

The stage interior is swathed in a warm Douglas fir and shares formal motifs with Gehry's Walt Disney Concert Hall in Los Angeles. Immense glass doors enclose the stage for temperature-controlled rehearsals and off-season events. The facility shares back-of-the-house space and rehearsal halls with the subterranean Harris Theater for Music and Dance that abuts the stage to the north.

Just to the east of the Great Lawn is the BP Bridge, an undulating, 925-foot, stainless steel Gehry confection that spans Columbus Drive with a gentle slope.

Contemporaine

Perkins+Will, 2004
516 North Wells Street

Concrete buildings of note in Chicago are few and far between. Most have been indicative of highly personal and idiosyncratic designers, Bertrand Goldberg and Harry Weese foremost among them. The Contemporaine is a different matter. Perkins+Will's highly accomplished Ralph Johnson drew upon the mass-produced legacy of architects such as Le Corbusier and Auguste Perret in this compact, fifteen-story, twenty-eight-unit apartment building in River North.

Johnson exposed each of the concrete floor slabs, including the canted decks of the parking garage, but most of the concrete columns were set slightly behind the infill glass facade. A series of small balconies and terraces create a rhythm across the elevations. Window mullions alternate to maintain the lively composition. At the corner of the building, a forty-five-foot column defines the entrance, and its height indicates the underside of the first apartment floor above. The tall column is reprised at the top of the building, where it is part of a multilevel penthouse unit.

Johnson used concrete walls to break down the building's mass into discrete pieces. The four-story parking garage directly relates to existing buildings on the block. A ground-floor store maintains the commercial nature of Wells Street.

For all the nondescript concrete apartment towers that have been built in Chicago in recent years, the Contemporaine is reputed to be the first exposed concrete high-rise to retain its raw concrete finish in almost two decades. The last architect to accomplish the feat was Bertrand Goldberg.

Hyatt Center

Pei Cobb Freed & Partners, 2005
71 South Wacker Drive

The curving, lozenge-shaped, forty-nine-story tower of the Hyatt Center breaks with the traditional boxy forms of most Loop high-rises. Built by the Chicago-based Pritzker family, who sponsor an eponymous award as the profession's version of the Nobel Prize, the building was the first Chicago skyscraper to be planned after the terrorist attacks of September 11, 2001. It incorporates well-integrated, high-tech security measures as fundamental features of the building.

Designed by Henry Cobb of the New York–based Pei Cobb Freed & Partners, the building is clad in continuous horizontal ribbons of glass and textured steel spandrels, punctuated by polished aluminum mullions. The concrete core echoes the lozenge shape and supports forty-five feet of uninterrupted column-free space between it and the outside wall. The curves allow for three-direction views from many office spaces.

A six-story bustle along the building's north edge reconciles its eccentric form with Chicago's gridiron and provides for separate entrances from both east and west sides of the structure. Small, well-planned spaces between the entrance and the lobby provide discrete locations for security monitoring equipment. The main lobby faces Monroe Street to the south and follows the long curve of the building's facade. A forty-foot-tall interior space with bamboo plantings has full-height glazing that visually connects this secure space with the outdoor plaza.

Consistent with the building's conception in a post-9/11 environment, large plaza planters are carefully positioned to prevent vehicles from approaching the tall glazed lobby walls.

Gary Comer Youth Center

John Ronan Architect, 2006
7200 South Ingleside Avenue

The Gary Comer Youth Center seeks to delight and ennoble its users while providing security and protection from its gritty inner-city neighborhood. The three-story steel-framed structure provides a permanent home for the local eight- to eighteen-year-olds associated with the South Shore Drill Team. Balancing the order implicit in a drill team, but striving to reflect a playfulness appropriate to their youth, the architect conceived a lively cement board–paneled facade speckled in a bright palette of reds and blues.

The building's facades have only a few windows, and most of these are bulletproof. But the interior lavishly uses glass to provide light and openness, fostering a sense of community and togetherness that is sadly lacking in the surrounding neighborhood. The central space is a dual-purpose lower-level gymnasium. Motorized seating unfolds from one wall to create a six-hundred-seat theater accessed from the first floor. The center's main spaces, including a cafeteria, a dance studio, recreation rooms, arts and crafts studios, and an exhibition/lecture hall, are located around the central gymnasium. Each is carefully planned so visual connections exist between multiple spaces.

A protected rooftop garden courtyard sits atop the long-span gymnasium space. It is representative of many ecologically sensitive "green" initiatives that twenty-first-century architects have adopted at the behest of Mayor Richard M. Daley. The low-slung, three-story building is capped by an eighty-foot steel tower sporting an LED sign. It provides information about events at the center and is a beacon for traffic up and down south South Chicago Street and along the nearby Chicago Skyway.

Index

Numbers in italics refer to illustrations.

Photography Credits

3: Photo by Steve Hall/Hedrich Blessing, courtesy of the Hyatt Center

4–5: Chicago History Museum

6–7: Anne Evans, Chicago Architecture Foundation

11: Chicago History Museum

13: James Steinkamp Photography

15: Chicago History Museum

16–17: City of Chicago/Peter J. Schulz

19 (top): Chicago History Museum

19 (bottom): Anne Evans, Chicago Architecture Foundation

20: Chicago History Museum

21: Anne Evans, Chicago Architecture Foundation

22 (top): Anne Evans, Chicago Architecture Foundation

22 (bottom) and 23: Chicago History Museum

24 and 25: Library of Congress, Prints & Photographs Division, HABS ILL, 16-CHIG, 24-3; Historic American Buildings Survey; Cervin Robinson, Photographer

26–27: Chicago History Museum

28: Anne Evans, Chicago Architecture Foundation

29 and 30: Chicago History Museum

31, 32–33, 34: Anne Evans, Chicago Architecture Foundation

35: Chicago History Museum

36: Anne Evans, Chicago Architecture Foundation

37: Chicago History Museum

38–39, 40–41: Anne Evans, Chicago Architecture Foundation

42 and 43: Chicago History Museum

44 and 45: Anne Evans, Chicago Architecture Foundation

47: Chicago History Museum

48 and 49: Anne Evans, Chicago Architecture Foundation

50: Courtesy The Frank Lloyd Wright Foundation, Taliesin West, Scottsdale, AZ.

51: Anne Evans, Chicago Architecture Foundation

53: Chicago History Museum

54–55, 57, 59, 61: Anne Evans, Chicago Architecture Foundation

63:Hedrich Blessing

65: Chicago History Museum

66, 67, 68–69: Photo by Robert Thall, courtesy of The Commission on Chicago Landmarks

71, 72, 73: Photo courtesy of the Commission on Chicago Landmarks

74–75, 76–77: Photo by Todd Eberle, courtesy of the Illinois Institute of Technology

78–79: Photo collage The Titanic by Stanley Tigerman, courtesy of the artist

80: Chicago History Museum

81: Hedrich Blessing

82: Chicago History Museum

83: Anne Evans, Chicago Architecture Foundation

85, 86–87, 88, 89: Chicago History Museum

90–91 and 92–93: Anne Evans, Chicago Architecture Foundation

94–95, 96–97, 98, 99, 100–101: Murphy/Jahn

103, 104–105, 107, 108–109: Anne Evans, Chicago Architecture Foundation

111: Chicago History Museum

112, 113, 114–115, 116, 117, 118–119: Krueck + Sexton

121, 122, 123, 124, 125, 126–127: Photo by Hedrich Blessing, courtesy of Kohn Pedersen Fox Associates PC

129 and 130–131: Anne Evans, Chicago Architecture Foundation

133: Photo courtesy of Judith Bromley

134: Photo courtesy of Tim Hursley

135, 136: Photo courtesy of Judith Bromley

137: Photo courtesy of Tim Hursley

138–139: Photo courtesy of Judith Bromley

140 (top and bottom), 141, 142, 143: Photo by Steve Hall/Hedrich Blessing, courtesy of Ross Barney Architects

145: Anne Evans, Chicago Architecture Foundation

146 (top and bottom), 147, 148–9, 150, 151, 152–153: Courtesy Booth Hansen Associates

155, 156–157, 158–159, 160–161: Steinkamp/Ballogg Photography Inc.

162: Chicago History Museum

163: Douglas Reid Fogelson Photography

164, 165, 166–167: Anne Evans, Chicago Architecture Foundation

168, 169, 170–171, 172–173, 174, 175, 176, 177: Photo by Richard Barnes, courtesy of Illinois Institute of Technology

179: City of Chicago/Mark Montgomery

180–181, 182–183, 184–185: Howard Ash

187, 188, 189, 190–191, 192–193: James Steinkamp Photography

194, 195, 196, 197, 198–199, 200–201: Photo by Steve Hall/Hedrich Blessing, courtesy of the Hyatt Center

202: Photo by Craig Dugan/Hedrich Blessing, courtesy of the Hyatt Center

203: Photo by Steve Hall/Hedrich Blessing, courtesy of the Hyatt Center

204, 205, 206–207, 208, 209, 210, 211, 212–213, 214–215, 216–217, 218, 219: John Ronan Architect